ināianei/now

Vaughan Rapatahana

ngā whakawhanaungatanga/ relationships

he papakupu o aroha

kāore he mātāmua

went to the urupā

knitting a poem

Invictus redux

ki te tūārahi

talking to my son in a funeral home

the gravamen

as I lose another

ngā kiritata hōu

to my wife overseas during lockdown

hā pīwakawaka

sixteen years

he papakupu o aroha

kāore he kupu ki tēnei reo

kia whakaahua i a koe.

e tarai ana ahau

kia kitea ētahi tūāhua.

kāore rawa.

mirumiru? he rite tangi ki te waireka.

mamahi? he pūhonga rite ki te kupu-ā-kaupapa

ki te kura.

ātaahua? pono, engari he kīwaha tonu.

ko 'he tangata pai'

i tua atu o te whakarehurehu.

pai ake kia whakarere

te kōpaki i a koe i roto i te tā.

kei te noho pai koe i tua atu

i te toikupu;

i tētahi ture tātai i te katoa.

kāore e taea e ngā arapū ki te hopu te aroha.

[a lexicon of love

there are no words in this language

to describe you.

I attempt

to discover some adjectives.

there are none.

bubbly? sounds like a soft drink.

diligent? reeks like school jargon.

beautiful? true, but so clichéd.

while 'a good person'

is beyond amorphous.

better to forgo

encapsulating you in print.

you exist well beyond

poetry;

any formula at all.

alphabets cannot spell love.]

kāore he mātāmua

auē Pereki

tāku tama ngaro

kei whea koe ināianei?

kua nui ngā tau anō

rite tonu ki ngā tūmatakōkiri

mā roto tāku roro whakamimiti

auē Pereki

tāku tama ngaro

kei whea koe ināianei?

katoa e toe

ko tēnei poroporoaki

ia kore,

he pukoro

whakahipahipa

pākia i ahau

ki nui ngā roimata
he rite tonu.

auē Pereki
tāku tama ngaro
kei whea koe ināianei?

kua heke haere ahau
ki tēnei tāruarua o te toikupu;
kāore aku mea kē atu.

[no primogeniture

o Blake

my lost son

where are you now?

it has already been many years -

like shooting stars

through my atrophic brain

o Blake

my lost son

where are you now?

all that remains

is this arrhythmic

obsequy,

an irregular

trebuchet

striking me

dolorous

every time.

o Blake

my lost son

where are you now?

I am reduced to

this anaphora:

I have nothing else.]

went to the urupā

[*he waka ianei e herea*: it's not a canoe that can be fastened.]

went to the urupā

to search for you.

some slabs were

waaaaaaaaay past

dead themselves.

they lay like

lachrymose lego blocks

a m i d s t the spinifex;

while the gorse camouflaged ghastly

god only may know what else.

the rain had given

its three-minute warning

sometime before.

& still you eluded me.

as its first outriders

captured me

       o v e r by the

                  irruptive wire

fence,

I wiped my moist eyes:

only a catafalque of clay

and flowers that might have been,

deigned to denote

          what you

              no longer were.

knitting a poem

I'm knitting this poem

for you. *knit 1 purl 2.*

found the pattern

in an old drawer

fraying at the seams. *knit 1 purl 2.*

I'm tatting together

a crochet

to keep us warm. *p2sso.*

cabling

a colourful coverall

to contain love. *p2sso.*

no *slip-stitched*

tangle here, *k2tog.*

only this

inter/twined/applique

taut to the touch. *k2tog.*

I'm knitting this poem

                    for you. *knit 1 purl 2.*

ribbing together

a cardigan of care

we can don

anytime our world

unravels. *knit 1 purl 2.*

I've sewn up

this poem

for you. *bind off.*

invictus redux

this was your favourite verse.

something I did not know

until   later.

far too late.

your life

revoked its rh^y th$_m$

rescinded its rhyme,

would never reach

crescendo.

we   became   fissured.

not masters of our fates

nor captains of our souls.

the kōrero we never had

the mokopuna we never shared

our future time together

a speculative fiction.

now only words remain.

a brusque poem

on bulimic paper,

wrenched from an aged book

lorn in a hick town library

no one remembers

but me.

ki te tūāraki

e mahara ana ahau i te rohe o tai tokerau

e mahara ahau i ngā rākau matomato

e mahara ahau i ngā manu rōreka

e mahara ahau i te rangi kikorangi

me ngā tuaone ki te onepū kōura

e mahara ana ahau ki ēnei mea.

engari,

te nuinga o ngā mea katoa

e mahara ana ahau i

te karera

te karera

te karera

o tāu mata,

    kei te takoto koe i tōku taha

i runga i tā māua moenga ruwha

i he ra wera rawa

        tūā*ra*ki.

    te

ki

[up north

I remember the northern district

I remember the verdurous trees

I remember the melodious birds

I remember the blue sky

and the beaches with golden sand.

I remember these things.

but

most of all

I remember

the light green

the light green

the light green

of your eyes,

  with you lying beside me

on   our   worn-out   bed

on a very hot day

        north.

up]

talking to my son in a funeral home

[*tiwhatiwha te pō, tiwhatiwha te ao:*

gloom and sorrow prevail, day and night]

I spoke more authentically

to you

during those thirty

etiolated minutes

than I ever did

when you were alive.

the stark room,

shaped more like a coffin

than what you lay in

quite composed,

unmoved by

my ascesis of angst,

my agenda of guilt.

the wooden floor

an eavesdropper

bouncing back a farrago

of belated apologies,

an echolocation

of mea culpa.

those faded walls,

the fake flowers in a neutral vase

and the box of tissues

supplicating for the tears

I could no longer summon,

during that one-sided

confession to myself.

the gravamen

I looked around the

concise chapel.

you were not there.

outside,

loading the coffin

weighted with gravitas,

I continued to s c a n

the tear-torn faces,

those eyes leaking grief.

you were not there.

I gravitate near the telephone.

expecting some avowal;

some concession that your

first-born mokopuna -

was   dead.

no message came.

there have been none since.

only this gravamen
wrenched
from within my soul:

you were **never** there.

it was as if
we were mere
remora,
nibbling nugatory
on your
more substantial
self.

burdened with your being;

a l w a y s

attending,

yet

forever

flailing

in your

                        absence.

as I lose another

the discontinuation

          continues.

an ex-lover

eschewing suicide watch,

her scarred wrists

palimpsests of pain.

a former friend,

hacking his

emphysemic path

toward quietus.

veteran uncles,

war-torn whanaunga

flensed of fear,

too aged to linger

          longer.

all metamorphosing

as they traverse

the orphic threshold

between bardo and beyond.

karakia

wane after a while,

slip away like

unguent fingertips,

like your grip on mine.

that last gasp,

those occluded eyes,

your body

a thin earthquake.

the uroboric void

replete

once more,

as I lose another.

ngā kiritata hōu

[the new neighbours]

the house

was a whale carcass,

filleted

   flotsam

        & jetsam

    here

               where

there   &   any ^

upside the corrugated

tornado

that was once a roof

he acclaimed us

every time,

'kia ora ki te whānau' -

his smile

an effulgent salutation,

his tattooed wave

of hammer,

a benediction.

below,

his comrade,

with bandana as bouquet,

performed CPR

on a door

dying in the rubble.

adrift the paraplegic

                    clothesline

a squad of red shirts

swung themselves dry

in the autumnal air,

  &

the cerise caps

doffed

to the truant boscage

seemed more frightened

by the scurfy gorse

than posed

any threat

to us,

as   o u t s i d e,

we strolled our dog,

a beast

far more mongrel

than any fading cryptid

embossed defiant

a c r o s s   everything

inside.

to my wife overseas during lockdown

no news from me today.

nothing to report.

walang balita mula sa akin ngayon

wala ng maiuulat.

the neighbours next door continue to party,

their oblivious festivity

fibrillating our thin walls,

while the other side might all be dead,

it has been so long since I saw them.

the sky hints at rain

but the sky here often lies,

straddling as it does,

this firmament of fiction.

I scan the screen,

for emails that make sense,

some scintillas of cogency.

this process satiates an hour   or two,

as I listen at l e n g t h

for any trilling blips

from the comatose phone

you once bought me,

somewhere else abroad.

it will soon be night here,

an excuse to bury myself in bed,

once more seeking sleep,

ensuring tepid time will trudge.

an oneiric escape route,

where ambagious dreams

have far more substance,

than anything these weeks

brought into being.

no news from me today.

nothing to report.

kāore he pānui nō ahau i tēnei rā.

kāore he mea kia rīpoata.

when you're not near

I am aeriform,

a semi-quaver

outside a tune,

      &

craving your return.

[walang balita mula sa akin ngayon

wala ng maiuulat.

This is Tagalog, my wife's first language.

It translates the lines immediately above it, that is -

no news from me today.

nothing to report.

kāore he pānui nō ahau i tēnei rā.

kāore he mea kia rīpoata.

This is Māori, my own first tongue.

It translates the lines immediately above, that is –

no news from me today.

nothing to report.]

hā pīwakawaka

hā pīwakawaka

kei whea koe ināianei

taku hoa iti?

he manu ki he waha rōreka

he whaikōrero pēnei i he waiata,

te taima katoa

he aha tāu kōrero e hoa?

he aha te tikanga

o tēnei kōwetewete karawhiti?

kāore ahau he mōhio

nō te mea kua nunumi kē koe

ki tētahi atu he wāhi

kāore ahau he kite i tāu whatu kanapa

kāore ahau he rongo i tāu pūrākau roa,

kua ngaro koe ināianei

me kei te ngere ahau i a koe,

hā pīwakawaka

kei whea koe ināianei?

(No copyright infringement intended).

[hey fantail

hey fantail

where are you now

my little friend?

a bird with a dulcet voice

an oratory like a song,

all the time

what is your story friend?

what is the meaning

of this one-sided conversation?

I do not know

because you have already disappeared

to another place

I cannot see your glistening eyes

I cannot hear your long tale,

you are lost now

& I am missing you

hey fantail

where are you now?]

sixteen years

[*whatia potatia te tihi o Taranaki*: the peak of Taranaki is
broken off]

kua tekau mā ono ngā tau

sixteen years have trundled by,

like a wounded locomotive.

had my bouts of breakdowns, break ups,

break throughs.

& came off the rails   then

                              and there.

your death still pervades,

my side-track maunder,

this erratic journey

through the tunnels of life,

across those ramshackle aqueducts

between stable station

& depots of disrepair.

misplaced my ticket stub decades ago,

never made first class.

guess I never will.

kua tekau mā ono ngā tau

sixteen years have trudged past.

& I'm still at that crossing.

those infernal bells never cease

                           their strident trill.

while the barriers taunt me

in fissiparous semaphore

                           that never fades.

your death is my own   l l f e l o n g   transit.

when I finally alight,

I pray you're waiting,

                           at the terminal.

ngā wāhi/places

taku maunga

te hokinga mai a Parihaka

ko aotearoa

mangakino

at lake maraetai

tolaga bay tapahi

common sense

birth 06/19

pampanga perspires octet

july in pampanga

to an american politician staring in the mirror

seasonal

kerikeri – ā mātou tāone, ā rātau teka

taku maunga

[*Hokia ki tau maunga kia purea ai koe enga hau a
Tawhirimatea*]

i ngā wā katoa ka ngau te āwangawanga

me hoki ahau

ki taku maunga

Taranaki

i ngā wāhi katoa

ka kurehu ki te hukarere

te kaitiaki mārohirohi

mō katoa i tēnei wāhi;

      me

aua hau hauāuru me hohoro

e whiuwhiu atu ngā here

kotahi taima me mō te katoa

tēnei wāhi tapu o oranga ngākau

he rite tonu ki te whakakitenga

e te whakapaia i ahau,

ia wā

ka kīia ahau ka hoki mai

ki te tāmata

i ahau ano.

[my mountain

43

[Return to your mountain, so that you can be cleansed
by the winds of Tawhirimatea.]

whenever the angst bites

I must return

to my mountain.

Taranaki,

omnipresent

looms niveous,

the majestic guardian

of all nearby,

    &

those swift west winds

whisk away the claustral

once and for all.

this sanctuary of solace

is epiphanic,

it catharsises me,

each time

I am called back

to reclaim

myself.]

te hokinga mai a Parihaka

i hoki

      ki raro

ki Parihaka

i tērā wiki.

i hiahiatia e ahau.

he iti noa te tūtei

mōnā he tūruhi koe

e kōpipiri koe ki he wakanoho,

he rōpū pōrohe rānei

o ngā kaihekengaru ngaro
ki runga i he whakatakanga nui
kūnakunaku
mō ngā ngaru tino momoho.

kua w h a k a n u i te urupā,
tēnā whakamaharatanga
whakamaumahara

i Te Whiti
kua kaha haere te māwhe,
me ētahi whare
ka rurerure ngā riwha hōu.

kei te marino tonu te wairua,
ka māhaki tonu ngā tangata o tēnei rohe,
ahakoa te mamae o te hītori.

   engari
ko ēnei he ārai
anake

i roto i tēnei marino ariari
i reira he awenga tūturu
me ahakoa he matakawa te hā,
e rongo ana ahau i te hira.

ko Parihaka
he hākari w h a k a h i r a h i r a,
i tōna tūnga monoa,
tētahi mea kia rongo te reka
ki a tātou katoa.

[Parihaka return

went back

       down

to Parihaka

last week.

I needed to.

there is not much to sleuth

if you are tourists

sardined in a campervan,

or a scruff of lost surfers

on a misdirected

bonanza wave

extravaganza.

the urupā has e x p a n d e d,

that obelisk

immortalising Te Whiti

has become more achromatic,

and some buildings

brandish new scars.

the atmosphere remains peaceful,

the people of this district ever humble,

despite the agony of history.

but

these are merely

camouflage.

inside this palpable stillness

there is tangible presence.

and while the tang is tart,

I taste the epochal.

Parihaka

is sumptuous s p r e a d,

its estimable standing,

something we all should savour.]

ko aotearoa

ko aotearoa te ingoa o tēnei whenua
ko aotearoa

ko aotearoa te ingoa o tēnei whenua
ko aotearoa

kāore tētahi atu a ingoa

ko ngā iwi Māori ngā tāngata whenua ki konei
ko nga iwi Māorl

ko ngā iwi Māori ngā tāngata whenua ki konei
ko ngā iwi Māori

kāore tētahi atu ngā tāngata tuatahi

ko he ingoa māori i mua i he ingoa rerekē
ko ngā tāngata tuatahi i mua i ngā tauiwi

āke ake ake ki ā mua hoki.

[aotearoa

aotearoa is the name of this land
aotearoa
aotearoa is the name of this land
aotearoa

not another name

the māori tribes are the first people here
the māori tribes
the māori tribes are the first people here
the māori tribes
not another people

a normal name before an abnormal name
a first people before strangers

forever and ever and ever in the time to come also.]

mangakino

[*ka mate whare tahi, ka ora whare rua*:

with one house, want; with two houses, plenty.]

residue of quondam

construction gangs,

      these

      rows

      of

      huts,

    s p i l l

the   village.

spaced   between   jungly   plots,

  some decrepit

                  a few refurbished

     several spasmodically

o c c u p l e d,

in this town without employ.

fulltime whare for local whānau,

manaaki whenua, manaaki tāngata,

& refuge for pensioners

marooned in the interstices,

all storing firewood

to forestall the cold.

.

nearer the lake

jut

    the moneyed ones.

huger homes,

cement drives,

an ostentatious boat or two

witness to their weekend jaunts

as part time summer-lovers;

finifugal in

shiny jeeps,

swanky SUV & trendy trucks.

he pai rangitahi

mangakino is our divide.

a magnifying glass

for our asymmetry

as a nation.

[manaaki whenua, manaaki tāngata – care for the land,
care for the people

he pai rangitahi – short term pleasure].

at lake maraetai

these swan

glide in

an ontology

alien to my own.

their empyrean metaphysic,

through all dimensions,

isomorphic

& immutable.

in their majesty

they t r a n s c e n d

   this lake

as they dip deep

  beneath;

as they glissade

with immaculate grace

  a c r o s s

the   surface;

as they foster

their   funicular of cygnets

in all directions.

this archipelago of swan

transubstantiate

my inauthenticity

into an ecstasy,

I could once

                never own.

tolaga bay *tapahi*

he aha ngā poro rākau kūwawa ai

ki runga tēnei one?

he aha ai?

ko te *tapahi* nui

nō te ono rākau

o tēnei rohe.

te moni ki mua te taiao

te apo ki mua te atamai.

he aha ngā poro rākau kūwawa ai

ki runga tēnei one?

he aha ai?

ko ngā poro nui

nō te ono rākau

o tēnei rohe

te moni ki mua te taiao

te apo ki mua te atamai.

ko he moumou nui

ko he paraiti weriweri

kāore he tangata e hiahia kia kite

kāore he kirikiri kōura ināianei

kāore he wāhi kia pārore

kāore te hī ika ki konei

ko te mutunga o tēnei one

kāore he one i te katoa

anō!

[Tolaga bay *slash*

why are there strewn logs

on this beach?

why?

it's the massive *slash*

from the forestry

of this region

money before the environment

greed before common sense

why are there strewn logs

on this beach?

why?

it's the many off-cuts

from the forestry

of this region

money before the environment

greed before common sense

it's a massive waste

it's an ugly blight

nobody wants to see

no golden sand now

not a place to relax

no fishing here

it's the end of this beach

it's not a beach at all

anymore!]

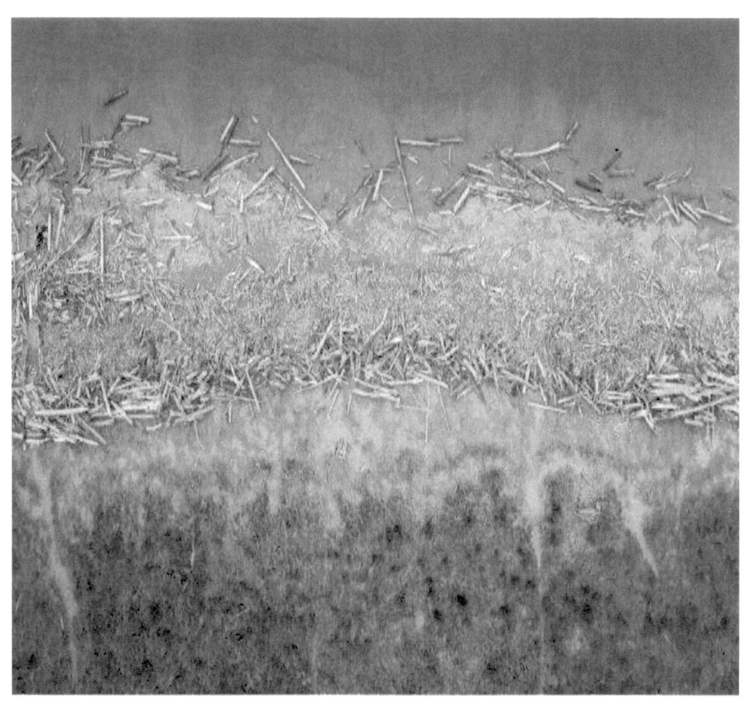

(**Photo credit** - Chris McKeen/Stuff)

common sense

hong kong does not do

senses too well.

some days we cannot see.

some days we sniff only the odoriferous -

                              so little ambrosial

here.

while all too often we taste only the nauseant.

there's too many of us at times,

as we do our best to avoid

touchingoneanother

on constricted footpaths,

inside concave malls

& *sardined* into the mtr.

the construction din in places is   traffic
over   traffic   traffic
whelming.   traffic   traffic

it   is   well   past   the   time

    we come to our senses

        come to sense

        come sense

            time

            now

            for

common sense.

birth, 06/19

we conceive birth as celebration,

an auroral awakening.

joy

justice

jubilation,

after months of angst.

we have staunchly survived

a difficult gestation

a harrowing propagation.

&

a nascent hong kong

is long overdue.

let us all now

gather conjubilant

for the nativity

&

deliver our progeny,

our prodigy

in style.

pampanga perspires octet

it's hot here today.

the wind is my enemy

and stays well away.

the geckos are sun-dried;

they clutter the floor

like broken tiles.

the fans try to assist,

but do little more than

stir fry the heat.

my brain lost traction

some time ago

and adheres in low gear.

no tradesmen ply

outside the iron gate:

the lane is dead.

it's hot here today.

the sun *smirks*;

our gleeful torturer.

july in pampanga

july was a   s l o w   month.

she refused to end.

every day seemed to linger,

each a simulacrum of the one before.

we dallied

we tergiversated,

she gave us sanction.

july was a *wet* month,

she spared no deluge.

every day seemed to rain,

each a facsimile of the one before.

we capitulated

we retrenched,

she gave us licence.

july said little,

she was pauciloquent.

every day seemed to stutter,

each a replica of the one before.

we quietened

we became agelast,

she gave us assent.

ito ay palagi mabagal

at palagi basa dito

such is july

in pampanga

[ito ay palagi mabagal

at palagi basa dito

- Tagalog –

it is always slow

and always wet here]

**to an american politician staring in the
mirror**

into the pulchritudinous vacuum that is your
soul

into the malfeasant maw that is your mouth

into the uxorious sponge that is your brain,

let us shovel some sense.

let us bulwark your steady cynosure

your constant grandiloquent self-reference

your endless anodyne bromide,

with unfalsifiable truths.

somewhere in the serpentine morass

that is your flabby flimflam,

somewhere in the profligate vacillation

that is your dilettantish haberdashery,

lurks some substance.

look in the mirror,

scan through the effulgence,

observe a human being

peering through the cracks.

seasonal

the sun has rung in sick

this morning;

won't be around today.

its nemesis has blown in

                            instead,

refuting the rules and roles

of canicule.

shitty sheets of rain

rebuke travelling outside,

ignore the fact

warmth & welcome

were supposed to

report for work.

it is climate change

in reverse,

summer running awol

& winter

out of season.

two upturned umbrellas

dying on the driveway

the symbol of

this existential antipode.

kerikeri – ā mātou tāone, ā rātau teka

['*On certain days of the week there are great congregations of Maoris* [sic] *in Kerikeri. They sit in parked cars and chat through the window. They buy fish-and-chips at the takeaway and eat it off butcher paper in the park. They splurge on lotto tickets, tailor-mades, pies with sauce, cream buns, and cases of beer. You can see them in the Laundromat, folding and gossiping while the kids play video games, or queueing up at the supermarket, their trolleys piled high with staples: flour in twenty-kilo bags, sugar, tea, milk, potatoes, pumpkins, butter, eggs, and jam'* from **Come on Shore and We Will Kill and Eat You** by **Christina Thompson** (2008)]

tihei mauri ora.

whakarongo

whakarongo

whakarongo ki te manu huia.

whakarongo ki te waha o te pono

ki tēnei kōrero whaitake.

whakaturi

whakaturi

whakaturi ngā kupu o tēnei pākehā

whakaturi ngā **hē** pohe

o tēnei kaituhi heahea.

74

ngā tāngata whenua o te rohe o kerikeri

kōwhiri i tā rātau e hiahia ana kia ora,

ina hiahia rātau,

te wahi e hiahia ana rātau;

a kāore he pēnei i tēnei moemoeā

ko tona wa kia **tūturu** mō ētahi tāngata mā

he tino rite ki ngā tāngata noho o tēnei tāone.

[kerikeri – our town, their bullshit

75

I claim the right to speak

listen

listen

listen to the huia bird

listen to the voice of truth

to this statement of fact.

ignore

ignore

ignore the words of this white person

ignore the blind mistakes

of this silly writer.

the indigenous people of the kerikeri district

choose how they want to live

when they want to

where they want to;

not like this fantasy.

76

it's time to get real for some white people.

real like the original inhabitants of this town.]

te hitori rāua ko ngā aituā o tēnei whenua/the history and tragedies of this land

he tino mā ā Kerikeri

he parekura: Ōrākau 1864

te korekore tonu

more

kei muri Ōtautahi

our men are killing themselves

te ngākau pōuri o te huaketo

ko te tāima mō he panoni nui

so let

when the utu came

flag this one

te pakanga nui o Waikato anō?

he mōteatea: huringa āhuarangi

so the theft continues

kāore ahau te kaikai ngā pākehā

(**New Zealand Herald** *One Roof* June 30, 2018)

he tino mā ā kerikeri?

part #1: keep it simple

you see the ad?

it's bad

what goes on inside the minds

of the clowns who compose this?

you see the ad?

it's bad

what is bereft in the brains

of the press who print this?

                                                you see the ad?

                                                    it's bad

2020 now/time to cease this shit

2020 now/no place for it.

part #2: mix it up

don't recall the place

as rampantly racist,

although the caretaker stated in 1978

that the homestead hotel

banned us 'til 1961.

don't recall any blatant

pākehā prejudice,

other than the occasional

middle-class

ruche of rolled eyes.

do recall the then languid

te tii and tapuaetahi

& my asking james henare

to judge the pei te hurinui

for the region in that same year.

do recall

multi-ethnic schooling,

multi-cultural citizenry   - and of course –

the usual quota of wankers;

as in any kiwi town.

kerikeri is very white?   he tino mā ā kerikeri?

not at that time   he kāore i taua wā

and hopefully,   me ko te tūmanako,

not now.   kāore ināianei

[Historical note: Vaughan Rapatahana taught at Kerikeri
High School 1977-79].

he parekura: Ōrākau 1864

[*'Women – many women – slaughtered, and many children slain, are amongst the trophies of Orakau, and "civilization" in pursuit, or as it returned from the chase, amused itself by shooting the wounded "barbarians," as they lay upon the ground where they had fallen'* (**New Zealander, cited in New Zealand Herald**, 15 April 1864.)]

I often drive sedately

to Ōrākau.

pause and ponder the plaques,

while my dog pees on the farmer's sterile fence.

there is not much there; the highway dis / sects the / site

like a brutal riposte

& the few *gnarled* trees

gather like gerontion waiting to die.

does anyone know what happened there?

does anyone care?

most cars zoom past myopic

while those sparsely parked there

are all-too-often mere

mobile phone cockpits

with sclerotic crews,

ready to zap back road ward.

does anyone know what happened there?

does anyone care?

Ōrākau was a massacre.

british troops bayoneted several wahine toa

mercilessly

as they lay wounded at the pā - and beyond,

when they fled outnumbered.

*I have had my fill of fighting, and do not care to
see any more, these poor killed and wounded
women have horrified me, and I am filled with
disgust, at the generally obscene and profane
behaviour of the troops.* (Interpreter William
Mair, 1865.)

the plaques do not mention this.

the small band of defenders were so staunch in
their resolve -

E hoa, ka whawhai tonu mātou, Āke! Āke! Āke!

& the sparse history tracts tend to ignore the
slaughter -

although a few now do set out the vitriol, the
violence

of those paroxysmal colonizers.

*Ōrākau, for instance, has been seen as a
glorious and noble and chivalrous battle. The
reality is that female prisoners were being
bayoneted to death* (Vincent O'Malley, 2016.)

when Ahumai made her brave declaration,

*Ki te mate ngā tāne, me mate anō ngā wāhine
me ngā tamariki*

she did not mean for Māori to die in such a
fashion,

even as she was shot four times herself.

Ōrākau was a massacre.

does anyone know what happened there?

does anyone care?

isn't it time, New Zealand, to learn about this in
school?

to stop shooting past the pā, like clowns on
cocaine?

to pause and to ponder probative about our
shared shame,

& the mamae thrumming still?

so we can then all move on.

[pā - fortified stockade/village

wahine toa - women warriors

E hoa, ka whawhai tonu mātou, Āke! Āke! Āke! Friend,
we will fight on forever and forever and forever!

*Ki te mate ngā tāne, me mate anō ngā wāhine me ngā
tamariki.* If the men die, the women and children must
die also.

mamae – pain, agony].

te korekore tonu

['By means of a thorough-going negativity, that which is
negative proceeds beyond its limits and assumes the
characteristics of the positive. While it does not entirely
emancipate itself from the negative, it does become
relatively positive'. **Māori Marsden**, *God, man, and
universe: a Māori view,* in *Te Ao Hurihuri Aspects of
Māoritanga* p.134].

āe, māori marsden,

ko te tino tika koe.

ko rua ngā whakakāhore

i mua te ao mārama,

i mua he ao o whakaora

mō ngā tāngata katoa.

ko tāku mahi

kia tuhituhi mō te wāmua

me nui ngā mea kino,

kia tauaro tēnei pōtangotango;

te korekore tonu,

kia taea ai e tātau katoa

e mataara i te ata

o he ao hōu.

[the void

yes, māori marsden,

you are quite correct.

there is a double negative

before the world of light,

before a world of healing

for all people.

it is my job

to write about the past

and the many bad events;

to face this intense darkness:

the real void.

so that we can all

witness the dawn

of a new world.]

more

āe, he pono..

ko aotearoa

taku tūrangawaewae metarahi,

engari

me mahi tonu ētahi atu.

in this country espousing equality,

I want to witness more.

    e pīrangi ana ahau kia mataara I ētahi atu.

in this homeland sanctioning sharing,

'diversity, kindness, compassion'

we must still offer more.

    e pīrangi ana ahau kia kite tēnei.

there can never be too much respect,

while love is limitless;

not some political somersault

flipped out when it suits.

the pith is this:

I crave even more

than we offer,

although we offer more

than our share.

      e pīrangi ana ahau tēnei wheako hoki.

me mahi tonu ētahi atu.

we must still do more.

[āe, he pono..

ko aotearoa

taku tūrangawaewae metarahi,

engari

me mahi tonu ētahi atu.

-    yes, it is true

aotearoa

is my wonderful homeland

but

we must still do more.

e pīrangi ana ahau kia mataara i ētahi atu.

I want to witness more

e pīrangi ana ahau kia kite tēnei.

I want to see this

e pīrangi ana ahau tēnei wheako hoki

I want this experience also

me mahi tonu ētahi atu

we must still do more.]

kei muri Ōtautahi

[after Christchurch]

after Christchurch,

scurried the disclaimers

'this is not new zealand.'

but it is.

it has been for far too long now.

we own, all by ourselves

- the highest rate of intimate partner
  violence in the developed world+.
- the highest death rate for teenagers in
  the developed world#.
- the highest youth suicide rate in the
  developed world*.
- the third highest rate of child
  maltreatment in the entire world*.

you respond with a

'terrible yes, but surely not as heinous as

the massacre at the mosque.'

90

whakarongo!

kei mua Ōtautahi

he maha ngā parekura

Ngatapa!

Handley's Woolshed!

Rangiaowhia!

all victims with the same skin colour,

all murdered by white men with guns.

ko Aotearoa tēnei

mō he tāima tino roa.

rawa roa.

[whakarongo!

kei mua Ōtautahi

he maha ngā parekura.

listen!

before Christchurch

there were many massacres

ko Aotearoa tēnei

mō he taima tino roa.

rawa roa.

this has been Aotearoa

for a very long time,

too long.]

[+Read *New Zealand Herald* 27/03/2017.

#Listen *to Newstalk ZB* 26/02/2019.

*See *Shockingly Bad New Zealand Statistics* online.]

our men are killing themselves

our men are killing themselves

our men are killing themselves

our men are killing themselves

our men are killing themselves

*the suicide rate among Māori men rose to
almost 32 per 100,000 in 2016*

our men are killing themselves

our men are killing themselves

our men are killing themselves

our men are killing themselves

more than double the non-Māori male rate

our men are killing themselves

our men are killing themselves

our men are killing themselves

our men are killing themselves

*the figure is the highest rate in the previous
decade*

our men are killing themselves

our men are killing themselves

our men are killing themselves

our men are killing themselves

*this rate has been steadily increasing for more than
10 years, and it seems to be getting worse*

our men are killing themselves

our men are killing themselves

our men are killing themselves

our men are killing themselves

it has got to stop!

te ngākau pōuri o te huaketo

(mō tāku tama)

kāore āku mea nui hei tāpiri.

he kaipatu te huaketo.

i roto i ngā āhuatanga nui atu i te kotahi.

ko ngā tohutohu anake ka taea e au te tuari

koinei:

me awhi tātau tētahi ki tētahi

pēnei kāore he āpōpō.

nā te mea ka ngaro tētahi puiaki

me te kore e tohatoha i tō aroha,

he kino ake i te mate ake.

[the virus blues

(for my son)

I do not have much to add.

the virus is a killer.

in more ways than one.

the only advice that I can share

                    is this:

we have to cherish one another

like there is no tomorrow.

because losing a precious one

without sharing your love,

is worse than the death itself.]

ko te tāima mō he panoni nui

ko te tāima mō he panoni nui ki tēnei whenua;
tāku whenua
ināianei

ko te tāima mō ngā whakaaro hōu
ināianei.

ko nui ngā rangatahi e mate whakamomori;

      he maha rawa ngā rangatahi Māori

ko nui ngā wāhine ki ngā patunga o te
whakarekereke ā-whare;

      he maha rawa ngā wāhine Māori

ko te kaupapa moroki o aukati iwi hoki;

      e mahara Ōtautahi.

he aha te raruraru kI ēnei tāngata ko kī tēnei
mauāhara?

he aha te raruraru ki ēnei tāngata ko te tino
kāpō ki titiro?

na te aha tēnei raruraru i te tūrūruhi ō mātou
ai?

he aha tēnei āwangawanga ki taku whenua?

kāore ahau he mōhio.

ko te tāima mō he panoni nui ki tēnei whenua;
tāku whenua
ināianei

ko te tāima mō ngā whakaaro hōu
ināianei

i mua i te mutunga o te wā.

[it is time for a big change

it is time for a big change in this land, my land
now

it is time for new thoughts
now.

there are many youths suiciding,

                too many Māori youths

there are many women as victims of domestic violence

                too many Māori women

there is the ongoing issue of racism also,

                remember Christchurch.

what is the problem with these people full of this hatred?

what is the problem of these people too blind to look?

why is there this problem of our inactivity?

what is this anxiety in my land?

I don't know.

It is time for a big change in this land, my land
now

It is time for new thoughts
now.

before it is too late.]

so let

talofa lava

namaste

malo

so let

ngā kupu

of any font/**TONE**/rebus

k   a   n   i   k   a   n   i

a   c   r   o   s   s

our   p a g e s;

f r

let the topos   o l

i c

amongst themselves, co-mingle, cross-breed,

counterculture,

coagulate

in   the   midst

o ngā reo

c a v o r t i n g   o n   t h e i r

o w n   f u n i c u l a r

so let   AOTEAROA

p

grOW   u   a   gear

he whakatupu nui

ki tēnei whenua:

mō ngā tāngata katoa

xie xie   salamat po

shukran

.

when the utu came

['Until the lions have their own historians, the history of
the hunt will always glorify the hunter'
- **Chinua Achebe**]

when the utu came

it was hypnogogic,

like those   gaudy   paintballs

           behind   your   eyes,

when you rub too hard.

when the utu came,

you had earned it.

merely by remaining caustic

awake   & somewhat aware.

your pen had done the dirty work:

it was up to readers

to scan intense

your sensate words,

to flit the message

on to designated others

simply by flicking the page

in their directions.

when the utu came

night-calling in its

open-mouthed finger-gibe

they knew,   as

                                        they

had always known,

they would wake as pariah,

pale castrato fingers snatching

at the jaunty sands

of shores no longer stolen –

if they ever woke at all.

[utu – reparation, recompense, revenge]

flag this one

'so,

why's that flag flapping

in your backyard?

        &

what is it anyway?'

the word florid had been invented to capture
his face.

tino rangatiratanga

'that's our emblem, brother.

it represents ngā iwi

standing up for themselves.'

'but that is not New Zealand's flag,'

he gave me The Gaze with eyes as BIG as his

overdue belly.

tino rangatiratanga

'too bloody right, e hoa

it's the standard of Aotearoa, eh'

'well.

it doesn't belong here...

our mawris are well-behaved;

they don't need stirrers like you.'

his fury was an app

for the existential prolapse

strewing & spewing

t

  his

    r

    toxicity

      u

        g

         h.

'hey, man, it's here to stay,

just like I am.

it's my flag, it's our flag,

                              fly

                                    ing

that's   why   it's   fly

          &

it   ain't   going   nowhere.

te pakanga nui o waikato anō?

1863-4

rangiriri, rangiaowhia, ōrākau
ko wai e mātau e pā ana ki ēnei?

kāore te rahinga
i tēnei whenua.

rangiriri, rangiaowhia, ōrākau
katoa i roto i tēnei takiwā

engari he torutoru ngā whakanui
i tēnei rohe.

rangiriri, rangiaowhia, ōrākau
roa rawa i mua e mea koutou?

kāo kāo kāo.

1981

kirikiriroa me awherika ki te tonga
ko wai e mātau e pā ana ki tēnei?

kāore te rahinga
i tēnei whenua.

kirikiriroa me awherika ki te tonga
te whakakore o te tākaro whutupōro

engari kāore ngā pakoko

i tēnei rohe.

kirikiriroa me awherika ki te tonga
roa rawa i mua e mea koutou?

kāo kāo kāo

2018

he aha te āhuatanga ināianei?
ko wai e mātau e pā ana ki tēnei?

ka kite a waikato
te mana taurite oti o ngā mātāwaka?

tērā rānei,
ko tonu te taua...

te pakanga nui o waikato anō?

[the great Waikato war, again?

1863-64

rangiriri, rangiaowhia, ōrākau
who knows about these?

not the majority
in this land.

rangiriri, rangiaowhia, ōrākau
all of them in this district,

but few commemorations
in this area.

rangiriri, rangiaowhia, ōrākau
too long ago for you?

no no no.

1981

hamilton and south africa
who knows about this?

not the majority
in this land.

hamilton and south africa
the cancellation of the rugby football

but no statues
in this area.

hamilton and south africa
too long ago for you?

no no no.

2018

what is the situation now?
who knows about this?

will waikato see
complete equality of the ethnic groups?

or then again,
is it still the same...

the great waikato war once more?]

he mōtaetea: huringa āhuarangi

kei te tino wera haere

kei te tino wera haere

kei te tino wera rawa ināianei

kei te piki ake te moana

kei te piki ake te moana

kei te teitei kē rawa atu

kei te haere mai ngā tauraki.

kei te haere mai ngā tauraki

ka noho rātau hei kaupapa mō ia rā

he waipuke tērā pea

he waipuke tērā pea

whakatakataka mō rātau

ko te huringa āwhuarangi ehara i te
pakiwaitara

tata kore he wā ki te whakatutuki:

ana mehemea kāore tātou…

e kāore tētahi e mawhiti ora

[climate change

it's getting hotter.
it's getting hotter.
it is too hot even now.

the sea is rising.
the sea is rising.
it is already too high.

droughts are coming.
droughts are coming
they will become a daily reality.
floods are likely.
floods are likely.
get ready for them.

climate change is no fiction.
almost no time to act:
& if we don't…
no one will escape alive.]

so the theft continues/ na reira ka haere tonu te tāhae

so the theft continues
- less manifest this
time around -
but still white fingers
in the cake, eh
 	
poking, ever poking
into the core
while licking off the
icing.
 	
our language was
stolen
our land was stolen
our lot was stolen
 	
it is PC now for them
to pray, to sing,
to bless the food
& to patronize with
obsequious palaver
and hollow words –
    including a few
words of our own -
about how best to
'close the gaps'
to 'accelerate
achievement'
to 'make full and fair
settlement'
	na reira ka haere tonu
	te tāhae -
	    iti te whakitea i tēnei
	wa huri noa -
	engari ano tonu maihao
	mā i roto i te keke, eh
	e wero tonu ana ki te
	iho
	i te mitimiti i te pani
	reka.
	
	i tāhaetia tō tātou reo
	i tāhaetia tō tātou
	whenua
	i tāhaetia tō tātou rota
	
	ināianei kei te PC ma
	rātou ki te inoi, ki te
	waiata, ki te manaaki i
	te kai
	& ki te whakaparahako i
	ngā kōrero patipati me
	ngā kupu huakore -
	    tae ana ki etahi
	kupu o tā tātou -
	mō te pehea pai ki te
	'kati ngā āputa'
	ki te 'whakatere paetae'
	ki te 'whakahanga
	whakataunga katoa, me

to 'equal up our Māori'	te tika', ki te 'orite tonu tō tātou Māori'
into good brown clones.	ki ngā pūrua parauri pai.
but	**engari**
our language is not widely taught *our land is not returned* *our lot remains the same.*	*e kāore te whakaako whānui tō tātou reo* *e kāore te whakahokia tō tātou whenua* *ka rite tonu tō tātou rota.*
so the theft continues a masque/psychodrama plaything a mighty falsehood even now 180 years f u r t h e r on.	na reira ka haere tonu te tāhae he huna/whakaari mea hianga he teka whakahira noa ināianei 180 ngā tau i runga atu.
our language was stolen *our land was stolen* *our lot was stolen.*	*i tāhaetia tō tātou reo* *i tāhaetia tō tātou whenua* *i tāhaetia tō tātou rota.*

kāore ahau he kaikai ngā pākehā

kāore ahau e pai he maha o ngā tāngata mā
engari kāore ahau e hiahia ki te kai i rātau.

kāore e taea e ahau te aro ki te maha o ngā
wāhine mā
a kāore ahau e hiahia ki te onioni i rātau.

ko he maha o ngā tāngata mā e hīteki ana
me o rātou upoku i runga ake o rātou whero,
me te aronga tino kōrori o te painga,
ki a rātau ko tō rātau reo nō te Atua hoki.

kāore āku wā mō te maha ngā tāne mā
me kāore ahau e hiahia ki te kōrero ki a rātau

kāore ahau e pai he maha o ngā tāngata mā
engari kāore ahau e hiahia ki te kai i rātau.

.

[I don't want to eat the pākehā

I do not like many white people,

but I don't want to eat them.

I cannot really stand many white women

& I don't want to fuck them.

many white folk strut around

with heads up arses

and have a particularly warped sense

of privilege;

they think their language

is also god's.

I don't have any time for many white men

& I don't want to talk with them.

I do not like many white people,

but I don't want to eat them.]

(Illustration -Pauline Canlas Wu)

ngā aurongo rāua ko ngā huatau/emotions and ideas

te huaketo tika 2020

kia atawhai – te huaketo 2020

two panko

ngā wāna

my turn approaches

coloratura

kōrero tonu i te reo

tongues

haven't had my fill

ko kerikeri he tūruapō

most my books

2020 boxes

existentially avian

mere speculation

he whakakitenga tēnei rā

god is a chain letter

caution

beyond dotage

the fool (Aotearoa version)

use the word

te huaketo tika 2020

[the true virus 2020]

after

driving myopic

25 kms through congealed mist,

like a pearl diver

too far down the murk,

I eventually

                        arrived.

the sole supermarket

aloof, doors sealed.

the carpark chained still,

a discouraging bulwark.

fresh-daubed lines outside

separated like hopscotch marks

in a kid's playground.

there we stationed ourselves,

a scruffy trickle

of small-town shoppers

desperate for some long-savoured item,

a few unable to sleep the early hours,

others, pensioners with first tilt

at what might remain inside.

as we stood by s p a c e d apart

we created an allegiance,

a harmony in discourse and jest,

our respect for one another

a flamethrower

to thaw the chill

and melt the indurate minutes

conspiring to forbid impetus.

.

eventually the cue

for the s t r e t c h I n g queue to progress

came from a staff member

lumbering a sign and sprays of sanitizer

while carrying a smile

that denied their labour.

we filtered in - the first wavelet

before the levee crashed -

smiling quickly as we stole the portico,

grinning in glee after our purchase,

as we bent back into the carpark

to sight an anfractuous array

d i s t e n d   into   the   distance,

yet still steadfast and patient

to wait their turns.

the only contagion we witnessed

was our regard for one another,

our pledge to overcome

this ordeal

through our own rapid virus:

some would label altruism.

I would call it

love.

kia atawhai – te huaketo 2020

kia atawhai ki ā koutou whānau

kia atawhai ki ā koutou whanaunga

kia atawhai ki ā koutou hoa

kia atawhai ki ā koutou kiritata

kia atawhai ki ā koutou hoamahi

kia atawhai ki ngā uakoao

kia atawhai ki ā koutou ano.

ka whakamatea te huaketo
ki te atawhai.

kia atawhai.

[be kind – the virus 2020

be kind to your families

be kind to your relatives

be kind to your friends

be kind to your neighbours

be kind to your workmates

be kind to strangers

be kind to people of other ethnicities

be kind to yourselves.

kill the virus

with kindness.

be kind.]

two panku

being locked do

              wn

    leads to

o p e n i n g.

s o c I a l

d i s t a n c I n g

   leads to

beingclosertogether.

ngā wāna

kei te roto ahau.

e kite ana ahau

i ngā wāna.

kei te ikiiki rātou i ahau.

ko he tangata kē ahau.

e tere ana rātou

enanga nei he merekara.

e pūmau whakahirahira

ana rātou.

ko te māoriori rātou.

e kite ana ahau

i ngā wāna.

ko tāku whakakitenga.

ko he tangata

pai kē atu ahau.

[the swans

I am at the lake.

I observe

the swans.

they transport me.

I am another man.

they glide

as if a miracle.

they exist

sublime.

they are serene.

I observe

the swans.

it is my epiphany.

I am

a better man.]

my turn approaches

as each day wilts,

I think more of death.

no despair here,

merely ageing

reflecting demise.

the existential

questions without quotient

more manifest;

the awareness

of ending

more obvious.

I read the news today, oh boy

& it's always dead set about dying:

storm, sinking, suicide;

all insinuating

my own approaching turn.

as each day wilts

I turn more toward death.

I need to welcome him,

before he strikes me unawares.

and though the news was rather sad,

well, I just had to laugh.

coloratura

be kind to your younger self.

they did not know.

be forgiving

of their foolish acts.

the ideals

deliquesced,

the hopes

submerged

by the seiche

of cynicism.

the bonds

busted,

the alliances

seized gelid

in the chill

of decennaries.

love

who you once were.

be generous

to that former self,

in a coloratura

to that unversed mimic

no longer gazing back

from the mirror.

kōrero tonu i te reo

['Mēnā ko te Māori te whakapae i tāu rātau ahurea
tuakiri hei iwi, me mahi e rātau i a rātau ake te reo
tupuna' - **Hirini Melbourne** 1991.

If Māori are to assert their cultural identity as a people,
they must do so in their own ancestral language.]

kōrero tonu i te reo

ko tāu ahurea tena

tuhia tonu i te reo

ko tāu ahurea tena

kāore wareware te pono o te reo Māori

ko te ngākau o tāu koiora

ki te kāore tāu reo

kāore e taea koe te Māori

[always speak your language

always speak your language

it is your culture

always write your language

it is your culture

don't forget the truth of the Māori language

it is the heart of life

without your language

you cannot be Māori.]

tongues

in the bedroom

my wife is talking to her mother

in kapampangan.

it is sultry this afternoon.

I am eating santol,

spitting out the seeds

into a plastic dish.

the rain pretends to come.

no one around here speaks english.

not because they cannot

but because they don't need to.

the weather here is trickster.

ako ay masuwerte dahil alam ko ang tagalog:

walang problema sa akin.

why should they prattle in an alien tongue

when I could learn their own?

in the salon

my stepchildren are conversing

in cantonese.

it is hazy here once more.

I am in the kitchen

chewing on the chao fan

splayed in a takeout box.

the rain feigns arrival.

no one around here speaks english.

not because they cannot

but because they don't need to.

the weather here is joker.

wǒ hěn xìngyùn, yīnwèi wǒ zhīdào pǔtōnghuà:
duì wǒ lái shuō méi wèntí

why should they prate in an alien tongue

when I could learn their own?

in the driveway

my cousins are arguing

in english.

the clouds hide the day.

I am in the garden

spooning out a kai

onto plastic plates.

the rain might soon be here.

everyone around here speaks english.

not because they must

but because they choose no other.

the weather tries to fool us.

ko he waimarie ahau mō he mōhio ahau tāku
reo Māori:
kāore he raruraru mō ahau.

why should I patter in an alien language

when they could learn my own?

the rain is now quite steady

it has chucked away its cape.

I poke out my tongue

to catch what it is saying.

[ako ay masuwerte dahil alam ko ang tagalog:
walang problema sa akin. – I am lucky as I know
Tagalog: no problem for me

wǒ hěn xìngyùn, yīnwèi wǒ zhīdào pǔtōnghuà:

duì wǒ lái shuō méi wèntí – I am lucky as I know
Mandarin: no problem for me

ko he waimarie ahau mō he mōhio ahau tāku reo Māori:

kāore he raruraru mō ahau – I am lucky as I know my
Māori language: no problem for me]

haven't had my fill

I wake up to eat

poetry for breakfast.

choose the words

from   a   clutter

of cartons

leaningtogether

on the shelf,

like students *stumbling*

their first

hotel session.

like them, I soon lose

my grip

as vowels

spill the fatigued carpet,

spelling out

auē

auē   auē

& different dipthongs

in other lexicons

I've yet to savour.

I   s t r e t c h   f u r t h e r

to grasp at

a jug full of fonts,

freeing arcane

examples in my haste:

esoteric

recondite

cabbalistic

soon

s p r e a d e a g l e
t h e   f l o o r.

the meal now

a   sch is med   skeleton
of

de   struc

        con   ted   s p a c e s.

            as

I remain ravening for **more**.

ko kerikeri he tūruapō

[kerikeri as epiphany]

I was younger then.

the sunshine sultry,

a deranged salesman

full-on and forever.

I was younger then.

the verdance dazzling;

a burlesque of purukamu

can-canning the highways.

I was younger then.

the yaws of yore a stanchion;

a stone store painted solid

onto the canvas of the river.

I am older now.

I reflect more than any mirror:

ko kerikeri he tūruapō,

a succour for my soul.

most my books

most my books concern

doomed men.

the limp pages

their lank arms

that never grasped

the tricks of life.

the fine print

never gleaned

by their inebriate eyes

& the worn spines

their jaded stance

toward early demise.

most my words concern

cloven people.

the schismatic sh at te r ings

their bro ken souls,

the arcane *stretchings*

of orphic lexis

their flailing hopes,

& the convolute repeats

their involute habits.

the body of my work

                    is an urupā

remote & elusory.

feel free to

discover,

drop in & delve,

never forgetting

to s p r i n k l e

              your wairua

each time

you clasp shut

the cover.

[urupā – burial ground

wairua - aura.]

2020 boxes

boxed-in?

got to think outside this box

no bubble

no social distance   got to stay

no kindness

no patience

                             outside this box

if we don't want to end up

                             in this box

existentially avian

I

a   m

al w ays

m o r e

authentic when airborne atop the clouds.

alienation

anomie

& angst

sink well

a sk e w

plunging

without

power

into

their own estranged

void.

mere speculation

just gotta tell you this,
before
you *slink*
          to sleep

been reading
vast tracts
this latest craze -
'speculative realism -'
with its antithetic rhythms
          of
re-defining-reason

[ivory tower dry balls
will just rankle it
as treason.]

my question – well
there's several –
would seem now

to be

'is quentin really real?'

or

is meillassoux

that lonely chair

maybe

l u r k i n g

over   there

or (again)

its hyperchaotic cousin

just   l i n g e r I n g   on the

stair?

he whakakitenga tēnei rā

i te taraiwa ahau ki tāku kāinga

tēnei ahiahi.

kei raro i te kōmaru tino wera.

e maire ana ngā manu.

i kāore ngā kapua.

me ngā kiritata?

kāore i tokomaha i tēnei tāone iti.

he māoriori ngā tokoitiiti kei konei,

me he pōhirihiri me he memene

i ngā wā katoa ka kōpikopiko ahau.

i te ohorere ka he whakaahuatanga.

te mutunga o te pahemo o te wā.

he marino i āpuru ana te wāhi katoa.

tāku roro ināianei he roto mākoha.

i he ihiihi tēnei.

i he mataora tēnei.

i he whakakitenga tēnei.

mahurutanga i kaukau i ahau.

i tēnei rā ko taku hoki wairua

hei tangata pai ake.

[an epiphany today

I was driving to my home,

this afternoon,

under a searing sun.

the birds were carolling

there were no clouds.

and the neighbours?

                not many in this small town.

the few here are contented,

with a smile and a wave

every time I ramble by.

suddenly there was transmutation.

time ceased passing.

tranquillity overwhelmed.

my brain now a calm lake.

this was ebullition.

this was satori.

this was an epiphany.

serenity bathed me.

today was my reincarnation,

as a better person.]

god is a chain letter

['No one has final authority over the true meaning of any text; not the experts, not the author' – **Jacques Derrida**]

god is a chain letter

    &

no one wants

to sever

this concatenation.

fear baulks them

@ every t u

        r n

as they trade

    in any

nous *pour un*

truc of an

intangible

nirvana   no one's ever tasted.

if they just keep

holding true

      to this missive

who knows

what

wonders

they'll

      witness?

prolific promises

abound,

e g r e g i o u s   in   the   e x t r e m e

   &   yet

with out

a semblance of sense

for any

sentient

soul.

BEST PRODUCT ON THE MARKET!

FULL   BRAIN   STAIN   REMOVAL!

MONEY   BACK   GUARANTEED!

NGĀ   TOIKUPU

Literary   Liquid   Soap

Puts   the   vim   into   rhythm

Puts   the   time   into   rhyme

(Ingredients: Lyricism 15%;   Cynicism 10%;   Idealism 10%;
Assorted Imagery 35%; Te reo Māori 20%;   Originality 10%;
Potential traces of Arcane Vocabulary and Wishful Thinking)

beyond dotage

as we stroll ever onward

time is a jester.

what were once,

innocent mishaps

muddy to aged atrophy.

sometimes I forget,

even further,

lapse,

linger pareidolic.

losing   it…

eyesight wanes purblind,

celerity wakes senescent,

arthritic fingers *fum ble*.

no metanoia this,

rather declination.

yet such devolution

never divorces,

the sole cogent constant

that is aroha.

a koha received, reciprocated,

replenishing,

even as the body

s

  t

   o

    o

     p

      s,

& then

ceases

its necrotic

stumble,

its cutaneous

crumble.

love o u t l i v e s

       all.

the fool (Aotearoa version)

['truth's a dog must to kennel; he must be whipp'd out' -
**The Fool, *King Lear*, I.4.640]

billy the bard

unsheathed well

his polysemous fool as a rapier;

his stance a sarcastic sabre,

a caustic cutlass

skewering us all.

domestic violence figures

no envied zenith

who are the fools?

youth suicide rates

our nation's shameful cicatrix

who are the fools?

stifling pollution cluster-bombs

s u f f o c a t i n g the oceans:

who are the fools?

corruption, criminality, poverty
global warming & warmongering,
who are the fools?

classism, racism, sexism,
extinction, pestilence, starvation
who are the fools?

afghanistan, iraq, north korea,   libel
somalia, syria, yemen   nauru:
who are the fools?

pity the fools
pity the fools
pity us fools

hubris

humbug

hypocrisy:

who is the fool?

vacillation

vacuity

vituperation:

who is the fool?

lost friends

lapsed chances

a dead son.

who is the fool?

pity the fool

pity the fool

pity this fool

aaaaaaargh

Aha!

I am the fool.

['the fool doth think he is wise, but the wise man knows himself to be' -**A fool, Touchstone**, *As You Like It*, V.1.2217]

(Illustration -Pauline Canlas Wu)

use the word

there is not enough use

of the word

fuck

in poetry.

never has been.

plenty about fucking

as couched in

allusive thrust & parry,

but not enough to

p

  e

    n

this dearth.

      t

        r

          a

            t

  .   e

we require, we need

more ejaculation of this word,

more blatant expression;

much more visceral verse.

much more requirement to

say something such as,

'that fucking politician

is fucking up our shared earth

and we are all fucked.'

how can we poeticize

authentically

if we don't give a fuck?

Acknowledgements

Most of these poems have been published, including in the following; some are forthcoming.

Landfall, Saltwater Love, Takahē , Fast Fibres, New Zealand Poetry Shelf, Poetry New Zealand Journal, Turbine/Kapohau, Tarot Journal, Fresh Ink Anthologies 2020 and *2021* (Cloud Ink Press), *Love in the Time of Covid Chronicle, Milly Magazine, Kei te Pai Journal; Flash Frontier, Ko Aotearoa Tātou We are New Zealand Anthology* (OUP), *Mayhem Literary Journal, The Perfect Weight of Blankets at Night Anthology* (New Zealand Poetry Society), *Nga Ripa Wai, Swirling Waters* (Pavlova Press), *Blackmail Press, Aotearoa Climate Change Anthology* (AUP), *Ka Mate Ka Ora A New Zealand Journal of Poetry and Poetics, Scoop Review of Books, This Twilight Menagerie* (Poetry Live Press), *Up Flynn Road, across Cook Strait, through the Magellanic Cloud* (Pōhutukawa Press), *New Zealand Poet Laureate Blog, Somewhere a Cleaner* (Landing Press).

No, Love is Not Dead: An Anthology of Love Poetry from Around the World (Chambers U.K.), *Modern Poetry in Translation* (U.K.), *These are Flying Islands* (Australia), *Otoliths* (Australia).

Devout Art and Literature (Canada), *Percutio* (France), *L'homme blanc est venu* edition bilingue anglaise et māori/francais (Les editions de la Tortue, France), *Danse Macabre* (USA), *Antipodes* (USA), Maverick (USA), *Poetry on Planes* (Ireland), *Coming to our Senses* (Hong Kong Writers Circle Anthology), *Puisi Dalam Zaman Tidak Puitis Malaysian World Poetry Recital Night Anthology* (Ministry of Tourism, National Library, ITBM, Malaysia), *Revista Prometeo 31st Medellin International Poetry Festival* (Colombia), *Poesys 24* and *Honeycombs* (Curtea de Arges Poetry Festival, Romania), *You Tube*.

(In Kuala Lumpur, 2019).

Vaughan Rapatahana (Te Ātiawa) commutes between homes in Hong Kong, Philippines, and Aotearoa New Zealand. He is widely published across several genre in both his main languages, te reo Māori and English and his work has been translated into Bahasa Malaysia, Italian, French, Mandarin, Romanian, Spanish. Additionally, he has lived and worked for several years in the Republic of Nauru, PR China, Brunei Darussalam, and the Middle East.

He earned a Ph. D from the University of Auckland with a thesis about Colin Wilson and writes extensively about Wilson. Rapatahana is a critic of the agencies of English language proliferation and the consequent decimation of indigenous tongues, inaugurating and co-editing *English language as Hydra* and *Why English? Confronting the Hydra* (Multilingual Matters, Bristol, UK, 2012 and 2016).

He is also a poet, with seven collections published in Hong Kong SAR; Macau; Philippines; USA; England; France, India, and Aotearoa New Zealand. *Atonement* (UST Press, Manila) was nominated for a National Book Award in Philippines (2016); he won the inaugural Proverse Poetry Prize the same year; and was included in Best New Zealand Poems (2017).

In September 2019, he participated in the World Poetry Recital Night, in Kuala Lumpur. Malaysia. In October 2019, he participated in the Poetry International Festival at The Southbank Centre, London. He also appeared at the Medellin Poetry Festival in Colombia during August 2021.

Rapatahana is one of the few World authors who consistently writes in and is published in te reo Māori (the Māori language). It is his mission to continue to do so and to push for a far wider recognition of the need to write and to be published in this tongue.

New Zealand Book Council Writers File is
https://www.bookcouncil.org.nz/writer/rapatahana-vaugh